PEACE WITH my Dad

GLORIA HICKS

Peace With My Dad Copyright © 2020 by Gloria Hicks

Published by Gloria Hicks

ISBN 978-0-578-74068-3

PRINTED IN THE UNITED STATES OF AMERICA ISBN:

Holy Bible, New Living Translation, copyright © 1996, 2004, 2007, 2013, 2015 by Tyndale House Foundation. Used by permission of Tyndale House Publishers Inc., Carol Stream, Illinois 60188. All rights reserved.

Scripture quotations from The Authorized (King James) Version. Rights in the Authorized Version in the United Kingdom are vested in the Crown. Reproduced by permission of the Crown's patentee, Cambridge University Press

Book Cover Design: Sophisticated Press LLC

Acknowledgements

With love and appreciation for all my siblings, our mothers and our entire family. We prove that love always wins. I thank God for allowing us the privilege to be examples of His love in action.

Foreword

As a child you are taught stranger danger but, sometimes life will arrange for you to encounter a genuine stranger that will change your life forever. Gloria Hicks was a quiet participant in my Author's class. She soaked in the information of the course because she had a story to tell. Little did I know, her story added to the volume of others globally crying out for attention from their daddies. They needed healing from these hurts by our Heavenly Father since physical Fathers sometimes fall short. It has been an honor comforting and communing with Gloria on this journey of reconciliation and restoration. Our common wounds of neglect during this pilgrimage to reconciliation made us no longer strangers but friends and fellow sisters in Jesus Christ. Gloria has beared the fruit of the Spirit through every phase. Always wearing integrity as an accessory to life. Her story provides hope that after the heartbreak of rejection and abandonment from those you love dearly there is redemption.

This redemption is obtainable and accessible if we forgive. Peace With My Dad provides the blueprint to forgiving Daddies all over the world.

Renetta Gunn-Stevens

CEO, Sophisticated Press LLC

Endorsements

I personally want to say how proud I am to see the finished product! Through many years of self-examining, struggle, and searching, this dream is now a reality.

May the pursuit of peace and accomplishment of this project catapult others to finding their inner peace, to make peace, and live peacefully with themselves and others. May this peace foster new and meaningful relationships and bring joy in the years to come.

I love you to life.

Forever your Sis,

Apostle Dr. Letricia A. Brown

Founder/ Senior Pastor of Kingdom International Ministries and Kingdom Ministries Church, Hampton, VA.

This book chronicles Gloria's journey through life, for many years without the presence of or relationship with her father. As time passed and they became better acquainted and she was introduced to sisters and brothers she did not know, she experienced incredible life changes. As if a light had been turned on within her, Gloria has blossomed into a remarkable young woman who is dedicated to God, her family and her church. I'm sure her journey with her father will bring blessings and joy – and maybe even guidance to some who find themselves in the place she was.

Dr. Evelyn Harper

As you read and go on this journey with this woman of God may it be revealed to you some answers, healing and deliverance that you have been searching for! A must read for Christians surviving today.

Dr. Sharon Holmes, Ekklesia International Ministries, Brentwood MD.

Gloria, congratulations on the publication of your book, "Peace With My Dad". I believe it will be a timely message to all who read what you have labored over as you put pen to paper. Further, I am certain this work will be a blessing to many. So glad to have worked with you in Women's Ministry, Intercessory Prayer and as Associate Ministers. You are my compassionate and passionate Sister Friend. Compassion for others, willing to assist whenever and wherever you can; and passionate about Ministry unto the Lord and His people.

Cheryl A. Stewart, Associate Minister Bethlehem Baptist Church, Alexandria VA.

Table of Contents

Introduction 1
Peace With My Dad 4
Importance of Peace 7
Making the Decision to be a Peacemaker 10
Peace Comes With a Price 15
Modeling Peace For Your Heritage 19
Setting The Right Course 22
Bibliography 26
About The Author 27

Introduction

On March 8, 2018, I received a terrifying call from my Aunt P, informing me that my Dad, LG, had not been heard from for a few days. This call was very alarming because Daddy lived in Topeka, Kansas, alone. My brother R, the relative who lived closest to Dad, was at least eight hours away in Dallas, Texas. I contacted the Topeka Police Department and requested a wellness check. When the police found Dad in the house, he had suffered a stroke at least two days prior. Thankfully, the room that Daddy fell in had a window that enabled the Police to see him lying on the floor. They broke into the house and found out he was still alive, but in critical condition.

Little did I know that this would initiate my journey of self-confrontation, repentance, self-healing, and prayerfulness concerning my relationship with my dad. This book is my reflective trek of making peace with my dad, and how important it has been to my life. I was blessed to connect, rely on, and bond with my siblings as we handled the responsibilities of caring for our father.

I pray that people who read this book will be encouraged and empowered to confront and address the inner conflicts that they may have. Often these types of hidden conflicts or turmoil are not resolved because they are traditionally taboo subjects. Unfortunately, the issues we do not confront still have a way of impacting how we see ourselves, how we treat others, and how we allow ourselves to be treated.

As a child, I was taught to be seen and not heard. Whatever happened in our house was not to be spoken of outside of the home. It would never have been acceptable to discuss my feeling betrayed, abandoned by my father, or being abused by people that were supposed to love and protect me. Based on this type of cultural upbringing, it is easy to understand how I remained silent when my paternal grandmother introduced me to my father, his new wife, and children via pictures. I visited her for the first time when I was 10 or 11 years old. During that visit I noticed pictures of people on her mantlepiece. I asked who the people were, and she told me. Although I kept silent, inside of me, the questions raged. "How is that his wife and kids, when he is married to my mom, and I'm his daughter?"

It is not unusual for the adult children of elder parents to have to care for and coordinate the care of their elder parents. I began writing this book while living through the experience of helping to make decisions about my father's treatment. My dad died prior my completing this book. So, you may notice the shifting from past to present. Prior to his passing, I had to help make decisions about Dad's rehabilitative care and subsequent end of life care. During this process I had to confront and examine my relationship with a man I had only come to know after I became an adult. Once a vibrant, intelligent, and handsome active duty Air Force man that lived his life according to his own rules. My dad had become a victim of life, age and sickness. Now life has brought things full circle, and it was he who needed and/or wanted me to support and help care for him. It is out of this crucible of faith, love and confronting legitimate feelings of "where were you when I needed you?", that this book was born.

The idea of being chosen by my Dad to share medical and financial power of attorney roles with another sister is mind-blowing to me. My life need for self-confrontation and examination is what prompted me to write this book. To my surprise, it has also been the tool God has used to help me to heal from the forces of abandonment, low self-esteem, and the lack of unworthiness that had plagued my entire life. I pray that as you read this book, you too will be healed and strengthened. I pray that you experience the love that God has for you, and how He designed you to be a vessel of love to others, even those who may have acted unlovingly toward you. It is the will of God that we prosper and be in health even as our soul prospers (3 John 2).

Peace With My Dad

My Christian faith causes me to believe that God utilizes all things to teach His children what His desire and will is for our lives.

Psalm 19:1-2 (NLT) states, "The heavens tell of the glory of God. The skies display his marvelous craftsmanship. Day after day, they continue to speak; night after night, they make Him known." Everything we experience in life is useful for us to learn of God's love for us, and to see His sovereign reign over all creation. There is a well-known saying that "our lives are God's gift to us; what we do with them is our gift back to Him." Everyone has received the opportunity to live life to its fullest, and to accomplish their God given dreams and goals. People can also experience life held in bondage mentally or emotionally due to the unfavorable circumstances that they have encountered. However, the outcome of soaring or crashing in life is contingent upon the choices we each make.

Greek philosopher Epictetus said, "it's not what happens to you, but how you react to it that matters." In examining my relationship with my dad, I realized that it was essential for me to make peace with the hurt I felt because of his abandonment when I was a child. It was never God's intent that the things experienced in my past would handicap or dismantle my future. Forgiving my dad, learning to accept him and appreciate the time that we had left, was a benefit to both of us. As a Christian, I have a God-mandated commitment to love and forgive my father and the sins he committed against me, even as I request Almighty God to forgive me of my sins. I realize that I may never forget or understand why my dad neglected me as a child. However, because of Christ, I am well equipped to forgive him and love him for just being my dad. It became my daily endeavor to love him and to appreciate him as my dad. Making peace required that I accept the fact that as a man, my dad did the best that he knew how to do at the time.

About eight months before Dad became ill, four of my siblings and I arranged a surprise trip to visit our father at his home in Topeka, Kansas. It was a beautiful trip. Some of my siblings were meeting each other for the first time. Although Daddy did not know that we had planned this trip, it had been his desire for us all to get together and to spend time with him. During that visit, Dad was able to talk to us about being abandoned by his father. He spoke about growing into manhood without knowing how to be a man or a husband because he had no example. Daddy apologized to each of us for not being a good father. Reflecting on my own life and many of the mistakes that I have made allowed me the wisdom to extend the same grace to my dad. After all, I wanted (and needed) God to forgive me for the wrong that I had done to many other people. During this trip, he had the opportunity to cook for us. Dad had had a stroke a few years prior to our visit, so he was unable to show us his championship bowling skills. But we had a wonderful time meeting some of his friends and bonding as a family.

One of the books that God used me to help in my journey of peace and forgiveness is *Developing a Lifestyle of Forgiveness* by Steve and Becky Diehl. If forgiveness is an issue that you struggle with, I highly recommend this book. According to the book one of the steps necessary to receive forgiveness is that "We learn to consider the losses we sustain from other people's sins. We need to learn to grieve over and mourn those losses appropriately, and then make healthy adjustments." (p.207) My decision to make peace with my dad did not mean that I ignored the fact that he had abandoned me. I decided to make the healthy choice of asking God to heal me and help me to love my dad, despite the sins of the past. Another lesson taught in this workbook is that the death of Jesus Christ on Calvary's cross was the only just sacrifice for man's sin. All of mankind's sins. As a child of the Most High God, I am to embrace the execution of Jesus as the full and just payment for sin. "Focusing on God, not the sin, will help you agree with God's just condemnation of every sin." (p.126)

Time of Reflection

Take a moment to reflect on someone that you have unforgiveness towards and need to make peace with. If there is not a person, then think of a situation that you have been struggling with.

1. What stops you from forgiving the person?
2. What do you gain by refusing to forgive?
3. What will you gain by choosing to forgive?

Spend time in Meditative Prayer about what you feel

How do you think God wants you to respond?

Perhaps as you read this book, there is someone that you have struggled with deciding to forgive them. Or you may be struggling to make peace with your past concerning things that may have happened to you. Be willing to forgive others just as you have been forgiven.

Importance of Peace

Merriam-Webster defines Peace as, "freedom from disturbance, or tranquility, a state or period in which there is no war, or in which war has ended." (Online dictionary, accessed on April 30, 2020) Christians have a biblical mandate to "Do all that you can to live at peace with everyone." (Romans 12: 18 NLT)

I believe that God designed the family as the crucible by which we learn about relationships and how to navigate our lives in context with other people. Family is also the human model for our spiritual relationship with God and the family of God, known as the Body of Christ. It is in our relationship with our mother, father, sisters, and brothers that we develop the pattern by which we relate to other members of society. Our immediate family shapes and forms our value system for others and our boundary systems for what we consider as appropriate or inappropriate behavior. Just as there are positive effects family relationships have on an individual's self-concept, there can also be adverse effects from negative family relationships.

According to Alexander Pagani, in *The Secrets of Deliverance*, "A father's words of affirmation can help his daughter realize her self-worth, but when that father figure is removed, demonic spirits will try to get girls to look for affirmation outside their home, even at an early age." (p. 113) I recognize that I had adopted some behaviors because of my relationship with my dad. Some of the behaviors that were affected: the lack of trust, hope, and love/commitment. Not only was I unable to trust other people, I felt I could not trust or love myself, as well as, feeling I was not worthy of love and commitment. In turn, my level of spiritual maturity was hindered by the unforgiveness I felt towards my dad.

The absence of peace in my relationship with my Dad caused me to limit my ability to trust and rely upon my Heavenly Father. In the context of our human family relationships, we develop our understanding of how to relate to God. Having the experience of being abandoned by my dad, impacted my level of trust (or lack thereof) in God. Without trusting God completely and without reservation, provided the enemy and my fleshly nature the tendency to try to control my own life rather than to learn to, "Trust in the Lord with all thine heart; and lean not unto thine own understanding. In all thine ways acknowledge him, and he shall direct thy paths" (Proverbs 3: 5-6 KJV).

From reading God's Word, I understood that He is Trustworthy, He is Faithful, and He promised never to leave or forsake me. (Hebrews 13:5 KJV) But now I recognize in real life, I did not trust God. I thought that God would abandon me, just as my Dad had done. Based on my experience, I felt no one could be trusted to protect or to provide for me because my family had never done it for me.

Hope is "a feeling of expectation and desire for a certain thing to happen, or a feeling of trust" (*Merriam Webster* online dictionary, Accessed on June 7, 2019). My concept of hope was rooted in my personal ability to provide and to protect myself. I knew that Psalm 43:5 instructed me to hope in God. My capacity to hope was viewed through the lens of unfulfilled hope in my parents and with other people. I had spent too much time interacting with God based on how I had learned to interact with people. I had extended hope toward people based on how I wanted them to perform. That hope was destroyed by their inability (or refusal) to respond to me how I thought they should act.

Biblical hope, also known as Christian hope, is defined as "the confident expectation of what God has promised, and its strength is in His faithfulness." (*Wiley* online dictionary, accessed on May 4, 2020) My ability to place my trust and hope in God was never about Him acting as I thought He should. It has always been about His faithfulness to His covenant with me as His daughter. God is faithful to His commitment and love of His people despite us and how we are. God, through Jesus Christ, proved that we could trust Him, our hope is secure in Him, and He is committed to us by this; "while we were yet sinners Christ died for us" (Romans 5:8 KJV). Learning to place my hope, trust, love and commitment in God and allowing Him to heal my heart and help me to trust Him to work on others has been the primary lesson of this journey of making peace with my Dad. I not only gained peace with my biological father; I learned to live in peace as a spiritually and emotionally mature child of God. By striving to live spiritually and emotionally mature, I am learning to, "Be kind one to another, tenderhearted, forgiving one another, even as God for Christ's sake hath forgiven you." (Ephesians 4: 32 KJV) I am Christ mandated to "do unto others as you would have them do to you." (Luke 6:31 KJV)

Time of Reflection

Spend time in Meditative Prayer

1. When you think of someone that you have struggled to forgive, what specific areas of your life have been affected? How have these areas been impacted?

2. What are you willing to do to achieve/receive spiritual maturity in those areas?

Making the Decision to be a Peacemaker

In Ephesians chapter 4, the Apostle Paul teaches that God has placed specific callings on our lives for the purpose of perfecting the Church. I believe that as parents and other family members, we are called (appointed) by God as gifts to each other. As gifts, we are to bless the lives of each other as we are examples of God's love to one another.

As we experience the gift of life with one another, we learn lessons from each other. These lessons may not always be acquired by a positive experience. However, the lessons are still being learned. If we allow God to be our instructor, we can learn the lessons and understand how His hand is working the lessons to our good and His glory. (Romans 8:28) The things we learn will bless our lives and equip us to assist and support others as they grow in their own faith walk.

As my parents prepared me for living in a global community, I was assigned to my children and my grandchildren to aid in their preparation for global community life. Making peace with my dad not only impacted my life; it directly affected the lives of my children and grandchildren. My adult children are aware of the relationship between my siblings and me. My children were blessed to meet all my siblings and most of their children and grandchildren. Our children have become so close that they travel across the country to visit each other and to vacation together.

My siblings and I wanted our children to know each other and to bond as a family. They knew the history of our lineage, which has helped them to appreciate the gift of love that God has blessed us with as a family. They have an enormous amount of love and respect for their aunts and uncles (no matter how near or far they may live.) Thanks to the availability of Facetime, Facebook, Instagram and other social media platforms, we can stay in connection with one another. Several of my friends are amazed at how well we get along because most of us did not grow up with each other, nor did we bond while we were children.

The bond and commitment that we have developed as a family was especially necessary in late March 2019. Our Dad had a severe fall, which resulted in hospitalization. By this time, we had already experienced the procedures and process of having to make medical decisions for him without an Advance Directive in place. Since his March 2018 illness, Dad had been to several rehabilitation facilities and decided that he wanted to go to North Carolina to live with his longtime friend, Ms. EC. Although my siblings and I, thought it best to have Dad complete rehabilitation in a center near where one of us lived, Dad and Ms. EC had other plans. Ms. EC went to Texas, accompanied by her daughter-in-law, and Dad signed himself out of the rehab facility, against medical advice. They had strategically done all this before any of his children could get there and stop their plan. So from August 2018 through March 2019, we traveled back and forth to North Carolina and coordinated with Ms. EC on Dad's care. In March 2019, when faced with the possibility of having to decide again what was best for Daddy, we all agreed that we needed God's intervention. Although Dad had reinjured the place on his brain that he had previously had bleeding from his March 2018 stroke, he was conscious, alert, and very cooperative. We had the chance to laugh at and with him about how he hydroplaned himself and his wheelchair off the front porch because he did not know his strength. He jokingly accused Ms.EC of pushing him off the porch. Thankfully, Daddy was well enough to execute his Advanced Directives, as well as, appoint my sister and I as his power or attorneys for both medical and financial matters. Both were done in the presence of our other siblings and with their agreement. Ms. EC was aware of Daddy's wishes, and we made it a point to include her in conversations that involved his care and needs. Dad was moved to another rehab facility for approximately a month so that he could get stronger, and he subsequently returned to home with Ms. EC.

At times, my siblings and I were frustrated and disappointed at times with Dad's behavior during his illnesses. We always found the God given grace to be patient and tried to make him as comfortable as possible. Often, we had to listen to his complaints about how we did not understand what was best for him, because he knew (according to him) what was the best thing for him. He was even disagreeable with Ms. EC and she had transformed her entire home and life to care for him. By the way, dad and Ms. EC had known each other since their days in high school. We are forever be grateful to Ms. EC for taking Dad into her home and caring for him. Wherever she went she took Dad with her. She would hardly ever allow anyone else to help care for him.

I am grateful to God for my journey to peace. It has allowed me to be an asset in the process of caring for my father. I appreciate being able to assist my siblings in this process by my knowledge of the healthcare facilities and legal process. Rather than being bitter, unhelpful, and uncaring towards my father and my siblings. I have the honor and privilege to share life with some of the most amazing people I have ever known, my siblings. There are two other siblings who, for their own reasons, chose not to connect. Thankfully, I am emotionally mature enough to not to take their decisions personally. I understand that everyone has the right to make their own decision on how they handle life. So, my prayer is that they have peace with whatever their choices are.

Deciding to cling to unforgiveness, bitterness and hurt causes us refuse to acknowledge or connect with our emotions. By denying our emotions we cut ourselves off from experiencing authentic life with ourselves, each other and with God. In fact, when we refuse to address/acknowledge our true feelings, often it is because we fear those feelings. It not unusual in the local church for it to be commonly taught or believed that acknowledging fear, anger, frustration or sadness to be an affront to God and is considered sin. This has caused many people to mask or hide their true feeling from God and hindered them from receiving the healing that they needed and desired.

According to Peter Scarrezo, in his book, *Emotionally Healthy Spirituality*, "the call of discipleship includes experiencing our feelings, reflecting on our feelings, and then thoughtfully responding to our feelings under the lordship of Jesus." (p.46) Refusal to disciple my feelings in accordance to God's Word had been my personal refusal to obey God's lordship over my life. This had hindered me from enjoying and embracing the life God intended for me to have.

In *Emotionally Healthy Spirituality*, Scazzero also states, that when he allowed himself to begin asking, "How do I feel about the church, my life, different relationships around me?" before God and others, it released a healing outpouring that not only set me free but everyone around me." (p.49)

Time of Reflection

1. What feelings or emotions are you aware that you have, but refuse to acknowledge?
2. What is stopping you from confronting these feelings?
3. What do you think that you will lose if you confront your true feeling about the things that have happened to you?
4. What do you stand to gain by confronting those feelings and allowing God to heal you?

Spend quiet time in Meditative Prayer

How does God what you to respond?

Peace Comes With a Price

In His pre-ordained plan to establish peace with His creation, God was willing to offer his only begotten Son as the sacrifice for our sins.

Jesus' willingness that we would have life and life eternal cost Him His life, according to John 3:16. Since Jesus is our example on how we should live, through our submitted lifestyle, we fulfill our obligation to God. 1st Corinthians 6:20 states, "For ye are brought with a price: therefore, glorify God in your body, and in your spirit, which are Gods." As sons and daughters of the Most High God, our lives belong to God. Just as children naturally look and act like their natural parents, our behavior and lifestyles should look like our Heavenly Father.

The price that I paid for choosing to love my dad and live in peace with him was to release him from the anguish and bitterness that I had felt towards him for many years. For as long as I could remember, I felt that I was entitled to dislike him. I thought that I had the right to be bitter because of the way he treated my mother and me. Deciding to forgive my dad also relinquished my ability to feel like a victim. I could no longer feel entitled to a pass because "I had no father image in my life." I could no longer use the excuse of being abandoned by my dad to live without holding myself accountable to live victoriously.

Making the decision to release and forgive my dad required that I take a good look at how I failed to apply the wisdom and goodness that God has blessed my life with. It also made me acknowledge that I had been my life's greatest enemy. Through much prayer and soul searching, these were a few of the things I learned.

Deciding to submit my life to God and desiring to take on His character and nature requires a complete lifestyle change. These changes begin to take place as I become committed and intentional in my determination to trust God and live according to His Word. It requires self-examination, self-confrontation, and acknowledging my low-level thinking. I had to ask God's forgiveness for my low level thinking, for not acknowledging His grace and love toward me. I realized that even though I had endured some hard times while growing up, God has always been present and faithful to me in the process.

For instance, I finally recognized that while I lived with my abusive aunt, God had blessed me with a guardian angel, our neighbor, Ms. Greene. I used to call Ms. Greene, Aunt Rose. She took me to church, exposed me to cultural events in the community, and showed me the emotional support and love that my aunt and my mother did not or could not. Aunt Rose traveled a lot and would bring back View-Master picture reels of the places she had visited. (For those who are too young to know what a View-Master-compare it to the modern-day PlayStation headset that you can play games with.) The reels allowed me to see the places Aunt Rose had been. The love that I received from Aunt Rose helped me to survive the four years of physical and mental abuse. During that time, I felt as if no one loved me enough to rescue me from my aunt. My mom knew about my aunt's abuse, but she didn't remove me from the situation. When my dad found about the abuse I was still living with my aunt, yet he did nothing to get me out of the situation either. For years even after I no longer lived with my aunt, I felt as if no one felt I was worth rescuing from that abusive situation.

One of the main lessons I have learned is people can only treat you as well as they know how. My aunt was abused and was extremely bitter about her own life. She was unable to treat me any better than she was treating herself. She had been in a longtime relationship with a married man who killed another man she had been dating. After completing his jailtime, my aunt and the married man continued to see each other, even as his wife continued to do "drive-byes" of our house. My aunt had also wanted children of her own, but never had any. My mom was afraid of my aunt because my aunt had previously assaulted and shot other family members. My Dad was emotional unavailable to care for anyone but himself. So, the expectation of being rescued by either of them was slim to none because neither of them had the capacity to.

I did not realize that my brokenness and not feeling worthy of love would eventually be a part of the reason that I ended up marrying a man, who was also emotionally unavailable, just like my Dad. Prior to getting married, I had not met most of my future in laws. I was not aware of my ex-husband's relationship with his own immediate family. I had no idea that at that time, neither of us could create a healthy, loving, supportive family for our children. So just as my parents had done with me, I did the best I knew how to love and teach my children to love others. Unfortunately, it was strictly love out my own brokenness. It was conditional, judgmental and its expression was situational.

Thankfully, the healing that God has given me addressed not only my relationship with my dad, but also the damaged relationships I had with my mother, my aunt, my ex-husband and my children. The healing process required that I forgive those that had injured me, as well as, to ask forgiveness of those that I injured, my children.

Receiving God's healing and deliverance in my life has relieved me from being a victim to the behavior of other people. It has allowed me to make peace and forgive my Dad and the others so that I can experience the best relationship of love and acceptance with each one of them. It has delivered me from feeling like a victim to others' behavior, as well as, helped me to realize I deserve to be treated well and respected, even as I respect and treat other people well. The standard for me to do the work of forgiving was set by the biblical mandate to treat others as I expect to be treated, in Luke 6:31. In all of this, I learned I had not been treating myself well. I had a desire to enjoy the life that

God has given me. I could only do that by obedience to Him, especially in the decision to forgive and make peace with my Dad and others.

Time of Reflection

1. As a result of what you have been through, who have you injured?

2. What have you done to repair those relationships?

3. How have the relationships improved?

Spend time in Meditative Prayer

How does God want you to respond?

Modeling Peace For Your Heritage

The decision to make peace with my dad has changed how I treat myself and others. Making peace based on the understanding that love is greater than hurt and unforgiveness. Love is founded in God because God is love. My three children-gifts God blessed me with, deserve to know and experience life at its best. Although they are all adults with their own children, I still have a God-given responsibility to be a model/example of peace to my family and others. My ex-husband and I were not the example of a loving family relationship that I wanted for my children. However, if there is life, there is hope. I hope that the difference forgiveness has made in my life will also impact their lives and their decision to forgive others.

Making peace with my dad enabled me to enjoy the relationship I had with my dad years before he got sick, and to help provide the best care possible for him after he became ill. The relationship my siblings and I have is founded on our personal decisions to make peace with our Dad. Although we did not know it at the time, we each had decided to enjoy the relationships that we have with each other and to love Dad. We each acknowledged that we had made significant mistakes in our own lives and have hurt others. That realization caused each of us to have greater compassion and patience with dad and ourselves. We treasured every opportunity we had to enjoy the time we had to spend with him each other.

Forgiving our Dad and making peace with him made the trips to Kansas, Texas, and North Carolina after he became ill, easier to do. We were able to visit him even when it was not an emergency. We visited because we missed him. Traveling to see Dad was made easier because of our love for him. God allowed me to make peace and forgive. This healing allowed me to enjoy the grace of celebrating the blessing of having my Dad still alive despite his injuries.

Wednesday September 12, 2019, Dad peacefully transitioned to his heavenly home. It was somewhat expected, but unexpected-so only three of us were able to get to North Carolina to accompany Dad to Cape Fear Hospice before escaping Hurricane Dorian.

The love and grace that my siblings and I had for my dad was evident in many ways throughout our journey together. Our outpouring of love toward our dad culminated and was evidenced at his memorial service. There was so much love and joy at the memorial service. We all experienced the same feelings of love, joy, peace, and contentment. It was the best memorial service I have ever attended. We purposed to have expressions of love and laughter shared, and asked attendees to share the same. The reflections and prayers by his grandchildren acknowledged that they were witnesses to the love and forgiveness of God. They witnessed based on what they had seen from us and our relationship with Daddy. The mothers of his children came and met each other for the first time. They bonded and have kept in contact with each other since.

Making peace through forgiveness is the best gift that I have given to myself and my loved ones. It has freed me to be able to love and embrace myself and enjoy life with others. Prayerfully and hopefully, my life and its example will help and encourage those who follow.

In *Conformed to His Image*, Kenneth Boa states, "The more we love God, the more we will express his transcendent love in others-centered deeds of kindness and goodness." (p.43) The active, unconditional love of God being manifested in our personal lives will effectively allow us the ability and capacity to love those people who we considered to be unlovable. Forgiveness is a process, that requires our intentional obedience and submission to God. The Holy Spirit enables us to rest and rely on the promises of God forgiveness as we submit ourselves unto him.

Time of Reflection

Speak to God in Meditative Prayer

1. What is the Lord saying is your next step on the forgiveness journey?

2. Are you willing to take the next step? Why or Why not?

Setting The Right Course

The journey to peace and forgiveness is a lifetime journey. That journey begins with sincere prayer and acknowledging our authentic feelings to God. The Holy Spirit who is the Spirit of Peace. He guides us in all truth. According to James 1:5 (Passion Bible Translation), "And if anyone longs to be wise, ask God for wisdom and he will give it! He won't see your lack of wisdom as an opportunity to scold you over your failures, but he will overwhelm your failures with his generous grace."

The practice of hiding and masking authentic feelings has held the lives of people hostage for too long. Families have failed, and churches have been made ineffective because people have denied themselves the opportunity to enjoy their lives. Refusing to allow God to heal us gives our enemy, our flesh, and other people power over our lives that they were never meant to have.

The meditative exercises that you completed after the previous chapters were designed to help start the journey to making peace with your past. The journey takes time, sometimes years. It involves the removal of layers of emotional damage. Be patient with yourself, make sure you remain consistent to the process. There will be highs and lows in this journey, but just keep going.

For example, in my acquiring peace process when I accepted Christ as Savior and Lord of my life at age 22, I wrote a letter to my dad apologizing for how I had treated him during the few times we had been in each other's company. For years afterward, I thought that I had forgiven him. It was not until I began to get ill every time, I had to travel to check on my dad and attend to his business affairs. I would become physically ill once I arrived where my dad was, or I would have to delay going to see about him because I was sick. I asked the Holy Spirit in prayer why was I getting sick. He revealed to me that I still resented dad for abandoning me.

Every time I would go visit him, subconsciously I was angry that although he had never come to see about me, I had to drop my whole life to go and see about him. Visiting him required purchasing airline tickets, paying for hotels and rental cars. During his last year of life, Dad was very insistent about wanting us to just come and visit. Due to our responsibilities as his power of attorney, my sister and I were traveling to see Dad every two months. Once I understood how and why I had these feelings, I asked the Holy Spirit to help me. I asked for forgiveness and healing of the brokenness that I had. Afterwards, the instances of sickness stopped. I am grateful for that healing because it was a turning point for me. I purposed in my heart to harbor no ill will towards my dad. I decided that my most important end goal was not only to forgive my dad, but also to ensure that I be an example of love, healing, and forgiveness to my family.

It is imperative to understand that there is an actual spiritual war between the Kingdom of God and the kingdom of darkness. The kingdom of darkness objective is to always "steal, kill and destroy." (John 10:10) The same verse lets us know that Jesus came that we would have life and life more abundantly. According to *Conformed to His Image*, "spiritual maturity is directly proportional to Christ-centeredness." (p.294) This means that our ability to gain spiritual maturity is achieved by our commitment to submission and surrender to Christ.

In *Emotionally Healthy Spirituality*, Sacrezzo indicates that like Job we must "trust the living God with the many mini-deaths that we experience in our lives. The central message of Christ is that suffering, and death bring resurrection and transformation." (p. 136) Relinquishing our own will and desires to honor and fulfill the will and desire of God are considered many mini deaths. Death to self and selfishness.

"Therefore, if any man be in Christ, he is a new creature: old things are passed away; behold, all things are become new." (2 Corinthians 5:17 KJV) As the Body of Christ, our relationship with God through Christ gives us all the newness of life that we all need. Our spiritual maturity is evidenced as we by the guidance of the Holy Spirit allowing Christ in us the hope of glory to live through us. (Colossians 1:27 KJV)

It was the Holy Spirit who revealed to me that my attitude towards my dad was sinful. In addition, it was the work of the Holy Spirit to soften my heart and help me to begin to see how all the negative things I thought and felt about my dad were against God's will for my life. It is through prayer, submission, and the guidance of the Holy Spirit that the course to healing begins and comes to its completion.

I have included the following prayers from Christian Word Ministries, *Book of Prayers*, to aid you in your journey to freedom.

Salvation Prayer

"Heavenly Father, I come to You now, I acknowledge You as God, Creator of Heaven and Earth. Heavenly Father, I confess that I am a sinner, I have sinned against You. I believe in my heart that Jesus Christ is Your Son and You sent Your Son to earth, and he was born a virgin. I believe that Jesus is the one true sacrifice for my sins. I believe that Jesus Christ was crucified on a cross as the sacrifice for the sins of the world, sins that have blinded me and separated me from You. I believe, Heavenly Father, that You sent Jesus Christ to personally die for me and my sins. I believe Jesus Christ, Your Son, took upon Himself all my sins and the sins of all mankind. I believe Jesus, who knew no sin, became sin for me that I may receive Eternal Life. I believe Heavenly Father, You raised Jesus Christ from the dead and He is alive and well, seated at Your Right Hand in Heaven. I now repent (turn) from my sins and choose to follow and obey Christ Jesus as my Lord and Savior. I ask you Jesus Christ to be the Lord of my life and lead me in all areas of my life. I receive you Lord Jesus as my Lord and Savior with all my heart and believe that You

are My King and My God. Lord fill me with Your Holy Spirit and use my life as a willing vessel. Heavenly Father I ask that my life will glorify You. Thank You Heavenly Father for my salvation by faith in Christ Jesus and the Truth of Your Word. In Jesus Name. Amen!"

Prayer of Forgiveness

"Heavenly Father, I come to you now in the Name of my Lord and Savior Christ Jesus. Heavenly Father, I forgive_____ _____ for anything that they have ever done or said to me, I bless them in the Name of Jesus Christ and I ask you to forgive and bless them in the Name of Jesus Christ according to John 14:14. Heavenly Father, I ask you to forgive me for any hard feelings I had toward them and fill me with Your love for _____ _____. I ask these things according to John 14:14."

John 14:14, states, "If ye ask anything in my name, I will do it." So, the blessing of our healing and deliverance is based on the credibility of God Word and His faithfulness to perform His Word.

Bibliography

Steve and Becky Diehl, *Developing a Lifestyle of Forgiveness: A Personal and Small Group Study Guide to Help you experience Healing, Freedom and Loving Relationships-2nd Edition* (Concord, CA: Forgiveness Ministries 2007), 126 & 207

Kenneth Boa, *Conformed to His Image: Biblical and Practical Approaches to Spiritual Formation*, (Grand Rapids, Mich: Zondervan, 2001), 43 & 249

Alexander Pagani, *The Secrets of Deliverance: Defeat the Toughest Cases of Demonic Bondage*, (Lake Mary, Florida, 2018), 113.

Peter Scazzero, *Emotionally Healthy Spirituality-Updated Edition: It's Impossible to be Spiritually Mature While Remaining Emotionally Immature*, (Grand Rapids, Mich: Zondervan, 2014), 49

"Hope". *Merriam-Webster.com Dictionary*, Merriam-Webster, https: www.merriam-webster.com/dictionary/hope. Access June 7, 2019.

"The Christian Hope". *Onlinelibrary.Wiley.com*, https://doi.org/10.1111/j.1758-6623.tb01593.x

"Peace". *Merriam-Webster.com Dictionary*, Merriam-Webster, https: www.merriam-webster.com/dictionary/peace. Access April 30, 2020.

Christian Word Ministries, *Book of Prayers*, (Lexington, KY), 119

About The Author

An ordained ministry leader, Gloria Hicks is a renowned teacher, Evangelistic and women's ministry leader, retreat and conference speaker. Having recently retired from her 32-year career in law enforcement, Gloria is currently establishing a non-profit transitional services program. She believes that God has blessed her to overcome the many adverse situations in life so that she can encourage other people. Gloria lives in Northern Virginia and enjoys spending time with her three children and six grandchildren. One of her greatest joys (and challenges) is attempting to teach her three youngest granddaughters to crotchet.

www.ingramcontent.com/pod-product-compliance
Lightning Source LLC
Chambersburg PA
CBHW070520090426
42735CB00012B/2848